P9-DME-804

To Porter ♥

*Ooops! Sometimes we make mistakes.*
*To find corrections to every issue of Block*
*go to:* **www.msqc.co/corrections**

# HELLO
## from MSQC

Fall is here! Summer is over and the kids are back in school. Our gardens are looking tired, the days are getting shorter, and our minds are starting to focus on quilts (If they ever stopped!). This is a wonderful time of year.

Lately I've been thinking a lot about creativity. Quilters have such spectacular imaginations. If I were to give ten quilters the exact same fabric, each one of them would come up with something unique, wonderful, and wholly their own.

Whenever a quilter shows me his or her work, I am quite amazed at the diversity and creativity demonstrated. Each of us thinks and expresses in a different way, and it is truly a joy to witness how much creative talent is out there. My ultimate goal is to encourage quilters to have the confidence to try something new. A project doesn't have to be flawless to be fabulous. Everything takes time and practice. Be proud of your journey, and remember, finished is better than perfect!

*Jenny*

JENNY DOAN
MISSOURI STAR QUILT CO

# warm *fuzzies*

Fall equals all things warm and cozy. The weather outside starts to feel a little more moody and the colors a bit more saturated. Inside becomes an escape from the crisp outside temps and opens its arms to recluse afternoons with decedent dark hot chocolate, a good book and a fuzzy, warm quilt.

When the days start to get shorter and temperatures lower in the evenings, a quilt is my happy place. And nothing quite compares to a quilt backed with a soft, cozy fabric like flannel. It's the ultimate snuggle-fest. When autumn cuddles up to you, I hope it finds you enjoying a quilt full of memories or inviting you to make new ones. Happy autumn!

CHRISTINE RICKS
*MSQC Creative Director, BLOCK MAGAZINE*

**SOLIDS**

**FBY19311** Primitive Muslin Flannel - Sunflower
by Primitive Gatherings for Moda Fabrics
SKU: F1040 12

**FBY17579** Woolies Flannel - Orange Herringbone
by Maywood Studios for Maywood Studios
SKU: F1841-M

**FBY19324** Primitive Muslin Flannel - Christmas
by Primitive Gatherings for Moda Fabrics
SKU: F1040 38

**FBY19315** Primitive Muslin Flannel - Pond
by Primitive Gatherings for Moda Fabrics
SKU: F1040 16

**FBY19316** Primitive Muslin Flannel - River
by Primitive Gatherings for Moda Fabrics
SKU: F1040 17

**FBY19331** Primitive Muslin Flannel - Grape
by Primitive Gatherings for Moda Fabrics
SKU: F1040 50

**PRINTS**

**FBY30006** A Mum for a Mum - Allover Mum Yellow
by Jackie Robinson for Benartex
SKU: 0612233B

**FBY26134** Melbourne - Adelaide Clay
by Andrea Komninos for Contempo Studios
SKU: 0609171B

**FBY28377** Hawthorn Ridge - Fall Leaves Barn Red
by Jan Patek Quilts for Moda Fabrics
SKU: 2163 14

**FBY28750** Sophie - Dot Blue
by Mary Koval for Windham Fabrics
SKU: 40823-2

**FBY2664** Lucky - Etapp Midnight Navy
by Lotta Jansdotter for Windham Fabrics
SKU: 40681-4

**FBY24128** Collections for a Cause - Mill Book c.1892 - Floral Bursts Purple by Howard Marcus for Moda
SKU: 46206 11

For the tutorial and everything need you to make this quilt visit:
**www.msqc.co/blockfall15**

# indian summer

quilt designed by JENNY DOAN

Like sands through the hourglass . . . so are the days of our lives.

When I was a young mom, I got in the habit of having the television on in my home. I guess I switched it on for children's shows and then it just never got turned off. Being at home with kids can be a bit lonely, and having adult voices in the background felt like company to me. When nap time came around and the kids were asleep, I would sit down for a break. There on the TV a popular soap opera was waiting for me. Before I knew it, I was wrapped up in the drama, and in a weird way the characters started to feel like my friends.

After a while I realized that between all the tension and theatrics on screen, nothing good ever seemed to happen. It was actually a little depressing. So one day as I sat down, I decided that I would keep watching the show only if at least one good thing happened in the story that day. Before I knew it, the one couple on the show that was still married announced they were getting a divorce. Ugh! I knew I should stop watching, but I wondered if I would be able to say goodbye to my TV friends.

That afternoon my oldest boy asked for permission to go with his friends to an R-rated movie. When I told him no he responded that if he wasn't allowed to see the movie, I really

shouldn't be watching soap operas every day. It only took me a minute to realize that he was right. I quit cold turkey.

Years later I was scrolling through the channels and stumbled across my old favorite show. I watched for a few minutes and do you know what? It was the same people with the same old problems and the same drama, and as for me, I would rather be quilting!

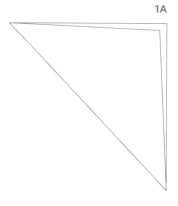

# materials

*makes a 70" X 87½" quilt*

**QUILT TOP**
- (1) pack 10" print squares
- (1) pack 10" background squares
  OR 3 yards cut into 10" squares

**BINDING**
- ¾ yards

**BACKING**
- 5½ yards

**SAMPLE QUILT**
- **Tiger Lily** by Heather Ross for Windham

# 1 block construction

Fold a background square once on the diagonal. Press the fold to make a crease. **1A**

Layer the background square with a print square with right sides facing. Sew ¼" on both sides of the crease. **1B**

Cut the square in half by cutting on the diagonal pressed crease.

Open and press the seam toward the darker color. Each yields (2) half-square triangles. **1C**

Fold one of the half-square triangles in

**1A**

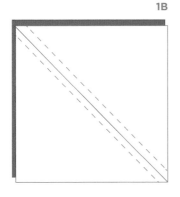

1B

half once on the diagonal. Press the fold to make a crease. 1D

Place the creased half-square triangle atop a matching half-square triangle with right sides and opposite colors facing. The seams will nest. Sew ¼" on either side of the crease. 1E

Cut the square in half by cutting on the diagonal pressed crease. 1F

Open and press the seam toward the darkest color. 1G Each yields (2) hour-glass blocks.
**Make 80 blocks.**

**Block Size:** 8¾" Finished

1C

## 2 assemble

Sew the blocks into rows of 8, alternating the direction of every other block. Make 10 rows. Press the seams in the odd numbered rows toward the left and the seams in the even numbered rows, toward the right.

Sew the rows together. 2A

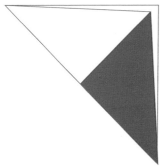

1D

## 3 quilt and bind

Layer the quilt with backing and batting and quilts as desired. Square up and trim the excess batting and backing away. Add binding to finish. See the Construction Basics (pg. 100) for binding instructions.

1E

1F

1G

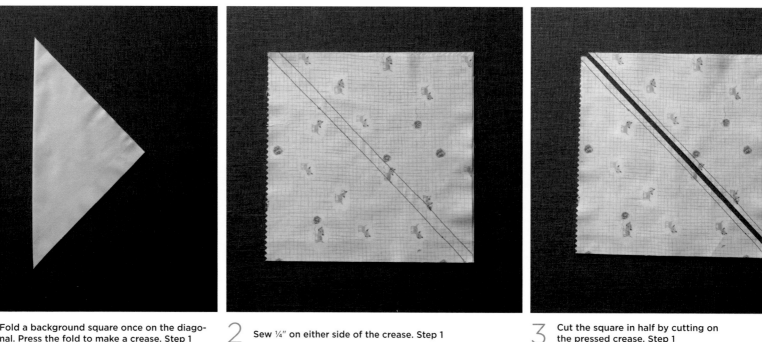

1 Fold a background square once on the diagonal. Press the fold to make a crease. Step 1

2 Sew ¼" on either side of the crease. Step 1

3 Cut the square in half by cutting on the pressed crease. Step 1

4 Layer a creased half-square triangle atop a matching half-square triangle with right sides and opposite sides facing. Sew ¼" away from the crease on both sides. Step 1

5 Cut on the crease between the two sewing lines. Step 1

6 Open and press. Step 1

14

# love notes
# *star*

quilt designed by NATALIE EARNHEART

When Ron and I had been married just a few years, I attended a class at church on how to improve our marriage. Things were great between Ron and me, but there's always room for improvement, right? I don't remember most of the tips they gave us in that class, but one thing I learned certainly stuck around for a while.

The teacher suggested that one way to keep the ol' flame alive is to leave love notes for your spouse. I don't like to do anything halfway, so one day I sat down and wrote about forty love notes and hid them everywhere I could possibly think of. Ron found notes in his shoes, in his lunch, and in the pockets of every pair of his pants. He found love notes for months!

Some weeks after my little love experiment, I went to watch Ron play in a baseball game. It had been a while since he last

*For the tutorial and everything you need to make this quilt visit:*
**www.msqc.co/blockfall15**

## love notes star quilt

played and he was having a devil of a time getting his mitt on. Finally he looked inside the mitt and found one of my notes! I could see a big grin spread across his face and he flashed the sign for "I love you" from his spot in right field. Boy did he get teased for that one, but later I heard one of his baseball buddies say: "Man, my wife never leaves me notes."

It was such a silly thing, really, but those notes reminded Ron that I love him. Heck, they didn't let him forget! That's the power of a quilt made with love. It's there on the bed, draped over the couch, or getting lugged around in the car, never letting you forget that somebody loves you. This quilt is definitely a love note that will stick around for a while.

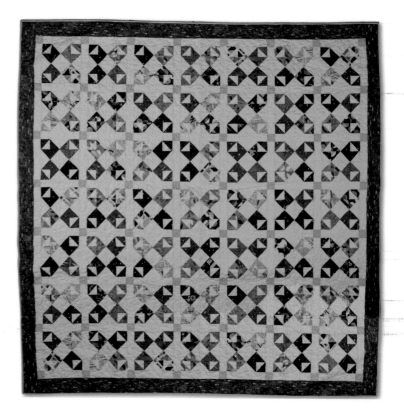

"It was such a silly thing, really, but those notes reminded Ron that I love him. Heck, they didn't let him forget!"

# materials

*makes a 82" X 94" quilt*

**QUILT TOP**
- 4 packs of 5″ print squares
- 4 packs of 5″ background squares
  OR 3 yards cut into 5″ squares

**SASHING**
- 2 yards background

**CORNERSTONES**
- ½ yard

**OUTSIDE BORDER**
- 1½ yards

**BINDING**
- ¾ yard

**BACKING**
- 7½ yards

**SAMPLE QUILT**
- **Story** by Carrie Bloomston/Such Designs for Windham

## 1 half-square triangles

Place a 5″ background square atop a 5″ print square, right sides facing. Stitch all the way around the outside of the layered squares using a ¼″ seam allowance. Cut through the two layers twice on the diagonal. **1A**

Open each half-square triangle and press the seam allowance toward the darker fabric. **1B Make 672.**

Square up the half-square triangles to 3″.

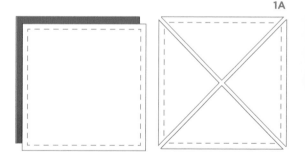

1A

1B

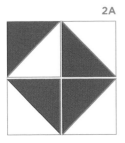

2A

## 2 block consterluction

Sew 4 half-square triangles together as shown to make one-fourth of the block. Make 4 units. **2A**

Sew the units together to complete the block. **Make 42. 2B**

**Block size:** 10″ Finished

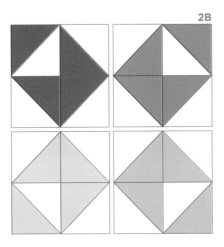

2B

## 3 cut sashing strips

From the background sashing fabric, cut:

- (25) 2½″ strips across the width of the fabric.

- Subcut the strips into (97) 2½″ x 10½″ rectangles.

## 4 cut cornerstones

From the cornerstone fabric, cut: (4) 2½″ strips across the width of the fabric. Subcut the strips into (56) 2½″ squares.

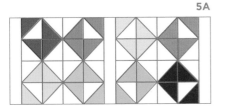

5A

## 5 arrange and sew

Lay out the blocks in rows, with each row containing 6 blocks. Place a 2½″ x 10½″ background rectangle at the beginning and end of each row as well as a strip between each block. Make 7 rows. Press all the seams toward the blocks. **5A**

6A

## 6 sashing strips

Sew a 2½″ square (cornerstone) to a background 2½″ x 10½″ background rect-angle. Add a 2½″ square, then another background rectangle. Continue on in this manner until you have sewn a strip containing 7 cornerstones and 6 rectangles. Press all seams toward the cornerstones. Make 8 sashing strips. **6A**

Sew a sashing strip between each row of blocks. Finish the center of the quilt by sewing one sashing strip to the top of the quilt and one to the bottom. **6B**

## 7 outer border

Cut (9) 4½″ strips across the width of the fabric. Sew the strips together end-to-end to make one long strip.

Refer to Borders (pg. 100) in the Construction Basics to measure and cut the borders. The strips for the sides are approximately 86½″ and the strips for the top and bottom are approximately 82½″.

## 8 quilt and bind

Layer the quilt with batting and backing and quilt. Square the quilt as you trim the excess backing and batting away. Add the binding to finish. See Construction Basics (pg. 101) for binding instructions.

1   Layer a 5″ background square with a print square. Sew all around the outer edge using a ¼″ seam allowance. Step 1

2   Cut the sewn squares twice on the diagonal. Step 1

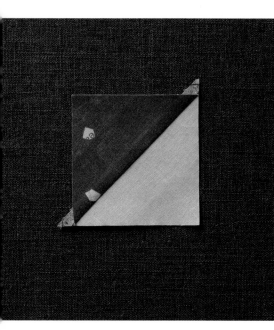

3   Open and press the half-square triangles with the seam allowance going toward the darkest fabric. Square each to 3″. Step 1

4   Sew 4 half-square triangles together to make one quadrant of the block. Step 2

5   Sew 4 quadrants together to complete the block. Step 2

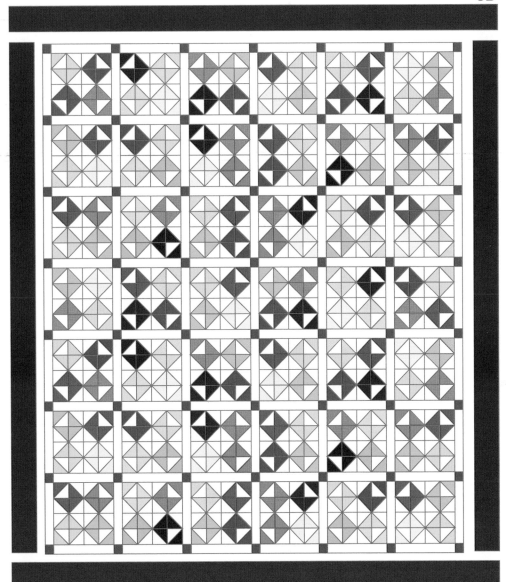

# flutterby quilt

quilt designed by NATALIE EARNHEART

Every October, thousands of monarch butterflies migrate to Pacific Grove, California in search of warmer climes. When we lived in California, witnessing this migration was one of our favorite things. I've never seen anything like a tree full of butterflies huddled together to keep warm. The butterflies perch in clusters on eucalyptus trees until you wouldn't know there was a tree there at all, just a giant tangle of colorful, fluttering wings. It's a stunning sight.

Monarch butterflies migrate south because they can't tolerate cold weather in winter, and they return in summer when it gets too hot. As you can imagine, butterflies are very delicate and they require a lot from their habitat. They come to the pine forest of Pacific Grove because there they can get everything they need: just the right food, humidity, shade, warmth, and protection from the wind.

For the tutorial and everything
you need to make this quilt visit:
www.msqc.co/blockfall15

## flutterby quilt

I don't consider myself particularly delicate, but sometimes I require a lot from my habitat too, and I like to get exactly what I need. Sometimes that means plenty to do and lots of creative stimulation. At other times I need a little quiet and some space to think. Most of the time, what I need includes a quilt, whether I'm making one for someone I love, admiring an antique with a rich history, or simply wrapping up with my sweetheart and a bowl of popcorn to watch a movie.

Monarch butterflies are pretty darn smart. Something inside them pushes them onward until they find just what they need to flourish. This quilt is a reminder to me of the those incredible butterflies and the importance of finding the things you need.

# materials
*makes a 57" X 69" quilt*

**QUILT TOP**
- (1) roll of 2½" strips

**BACKGROUND AND INNER BORDER**
- 1¼ yards

**OUTER BORDER**
- 1¼ yards

**BINDING**
- ¾ yard

**BACKING**
- 3¾ yards

**SAMPLE QUILT**
- **Small Talk** by Studio E

## 1 cut

From the background fabric, cut:
(8) 2½" strips across the width of the fabric.
Subcut the strips into 2½" squares for a total of 126.

Select 32 strips from the roll. From each strip, cut:

- (6) 2½" squares

- (4) 2½" x 6½" rectangles

2A

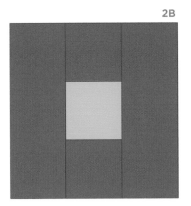
2B

## 2 sew

Sew a 2½" square to the top and bottom of a contrasting 2½" square. **2A**

Sew a matching 2½" x 6½" strip to either side of the center of the block. **2B**

Fold (2) 2½" corner squares in half once on the diagonal and press a crease on the fold line. The crease will be your sewing line. **2C**

2C

Place a square on one corner of the block with right sides facing and stitch on the crease. Repeat for the opposing corner of the block.

Trim ¼" away from the sewn seam and press. **Make 63. 2D**

**Block Size**: 6" Finished

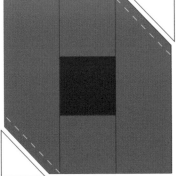
2D

## 3 layout rows

Sew the blocks together into rows of 7. Make 9 rows. Press the seams of the even rows toward the left and the odd rows toward the right to make the seams nest. **3A** (see on pg. 4)

## 4 inner borders

Cut (6) 2½" strips across the width of the fabric. Sew the strips together end-to-end to make one long strip.

Refer to Borders (pg. 100) in the Construction Basics to measure and cut the borders. The strips for the sides are approximately 54½" and the strips for the top and bottom are approximately 46½".

## 5 outer border

Cut (7) 6" strips across the width of the fabric. Sew the strips together end-to-end to make one long strip.

Again, refer to Borders (pg. 100) in the Construction Basics to measure and cut the borders. The strips for the sides are approximately 58½" and the strips for the top and bottom are approximately 57½".

## 6 quilt and bind

Layer the quilt with batting and backing and quilt. Square the quilt as you trim the excess backing and batting away. Add the binding to finish. See Construction Basics (pg. 101) for binding instructions.

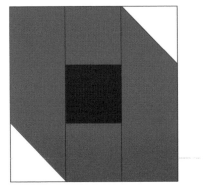
2E

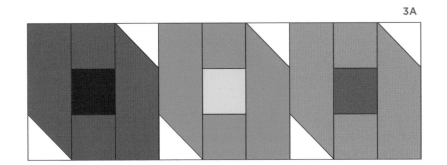
3A

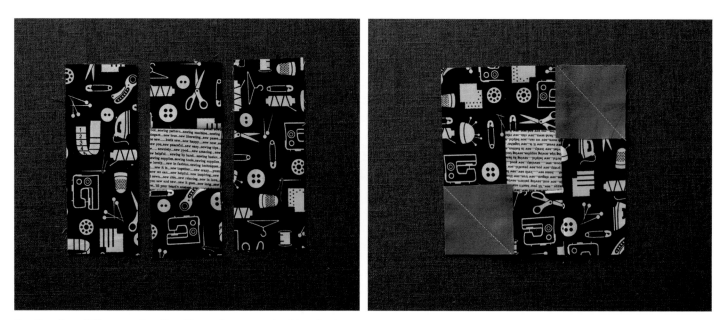

1 Sew three 2½" squares together. The center square should contrast with the outer squares. Sew a 2½" x 6½" strip to either side of the pieced center. Step 2

2 Sew a 2½" background square to two opposing corners. Step 2.

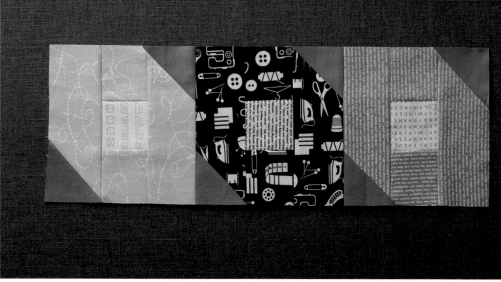

3 Press after trimming the corners. Step 2

4 Sew the blocks together into rows. Step 3

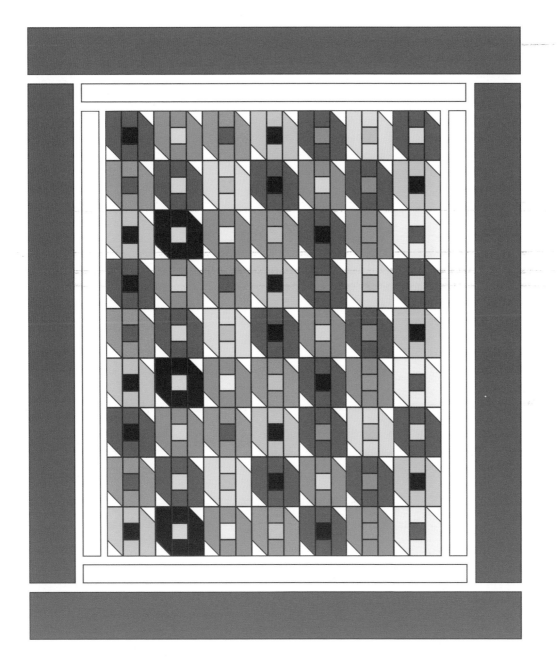

# *hashtag* quilt

quilt designed by JENNY DOAN

Methods of communication have changed drastically over the
past hundred years. Do you remember the days when letter
writing was almost an art? My friend's grandmother had a box
filled with correspondence from her mother, her sisters, and
best of all, from my friend's grandfather, who wrote dozens
of love letters from his stations on small islands all across
the Pacific during World War II. These letters are a treasure
of information. Reading them is like getting a glimpse of
what life was like during the 1940s. And the penmanship was
simply divine! I just can't get enough of the delicate curls and
flourishes of carefully perfected cursive. Nowadays most of
us type much more than we write (and for some, emoji have
replaced words altogether), and I've noticed that oftentimes
our penmanship is much closer to chicken scratch than the
elegant calligraphy of generations past.

*For the tutorial and everything
you need to make this quilt visit:*
**www.msqc.co/blockfall15**

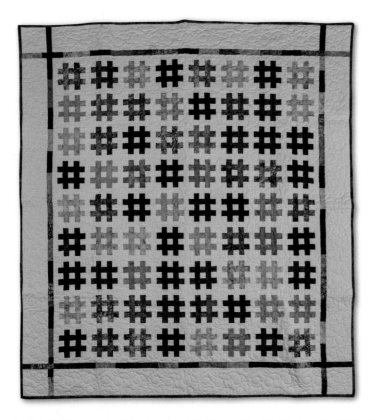

Sadly, these days it's rare to find a handwritten letter in the mailbox. Everything is printed and very little of it involves interpersonal communication. Instead, we get bills and direct mailings. But it's not just letters that have gone out of fashion. Consider how different phone use is for our kids than it was for our parents.

When my mom was young, her home had a phone, but it was a party line. In other words, my mom's family shared one phone line with the neighbors. Each household had a distinct ring, so when the phone rang, you had to pay attention to make sure the call was for you! And because the line was shared, you could pick up the phone to call a friend only to discover that Mrs. Smith down the lane was already chatting up a storm, and then you'd have to wait for her conversation to end before you could make your call!

Today, not only do we all have our very own phone lines, but you'd be hard pressed to find anyone above the age of twelve who doesn't also have a cellphone in their pocket at all times!

And those phones aren't just for calling. They are for emailing, texting, taking photos, playing games, and so much more. Your "phone" is now a portal to the entire world. We've come a long way from handwritten letters and the telegraph.

The Hashtag Quilt is a fun reminder of how quickly things have changed in the world of communication. What once was known as the pound sign or the number sign has now become one of the most unique elements of modern communication: the hashtag, a way of linking to other messages of similar theme or content. Sometimes I feel a little lost in the world of "tweets" and "insta" this-and-that, but I have to admit, it sure is amazing the way we can connect and share ideas across the globe with just the press of a few buttons. #istillcallitthepoundsign #hoorayfortechnology #whatwilltheycomeupwithnext.

# materials

*makes an 61" X 67" quilt*

**QUILT TOP**
• 1 package 10" print squares

**BACKGROUND AND BORDERS**
• 3½ yards

**BINDING**
• ½ yard

**BACKING**
• 4 yards

**SAMPLE QUILT**
• **Malam Batiks Blueberry Plum** by
Jinny Beyer for RJR

## 1 cut

Cut the print 10" squares into 1½" strips.
You'll need 72 strips for the pieced strip
sets. Trim 144 strips to 1½" x 5½" for the
blocks. Set aside leftovers from trimming and all other strips to use in the
borders.

 **Note:** *You can either mix or match
your strips. One 10" square can be
used to make 2 blocks. (2) 1½" x 10"
strips are used for the pieced strip
set and the other (4) are trimmed
to 1½" x 5½" for the 2 blocks. The
remaining pieces are used for the
borders.*

2A
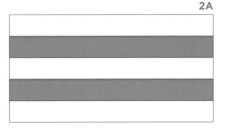

2B
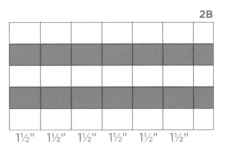

1½"  1½"  1½"  1½"  1½"  1½"

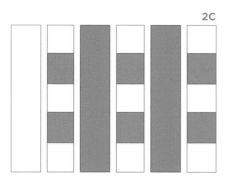

**2C**

From the background fabric, cut:
- (108) 1½" x 10" strips
- (72) 1½" x 5½" strips
- (72) 1½" x 6½" strips

## 2 sew

Sew three background strips to two print strips. Alternate the background strips with the print strips. Press toward the darkest fabric.

**Make 36 strip sets.** 2A

Cut the strip set you have just sewn into (6) 1½" increments. 2B

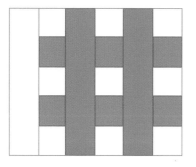

Sew a strip set to a background 1½" x 5½" strip. Add a print strip and follow it with a strip set Add another print strip. End with a strip set as shown. Press toward the darkest fabric. 2C

Sew a background 1½" x 6½" strip to the bottom to complete the block. **Make 72.** 2D (See 2A-2D diagrams)

**Block size:** 6" Finished

## 3 arrange and sew

Arrange the blocks to your satisfaction and sew into rows of 8. Make 9 rows. Press the seam allowances of all odd numbered rows toward the left and all even numbered rows toward the right.

Sew the rows together to complete the center of the quilt.

**2D**

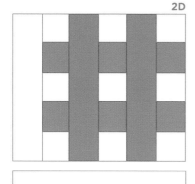

## 4 inner border

Cut (3) 1½" strips across the width of the background fabric. Sew the strips end-to-end to make one long strip. Notice this border only goes on one side and the top of the quilt.

Measure the quilt through the center vertically in three different places, always staying away from the edges. Cut one strip to that measurement (approximately 54½") and sew it to the right side of the quilt.

Measure the quilt through the center horizontally using the same technique as above. Cut one strip to that measurement (approximately 49½") and sew it to the top of the quilt.

## 5 outer border

We are going to do the two outer borders differently than usual. It's very important to measure accurately when making borders using this method.

Measure the quilt vertically through the center in three different places staying away from the outside edges. Sew enough 1½" print strips to equal that measurement (approximately 55½"). Set aside for the moment.

Make (2) 5½" background border strips that same measurement. Sew a print pieced strip to each of these wider background strips. Press the seam allowances

1  Cut the strip sets into 1½″ increments. Step 2

2  Sew a background strip to a strip set. Add a print strip, followed by strip set. Stitch another print strip and a strip set in place. Step 2

3  Sew a 1½″ x 6½″ background strip to the bottom to complete the block. Step 2

4  Sew the blocks together into rows. Step 3

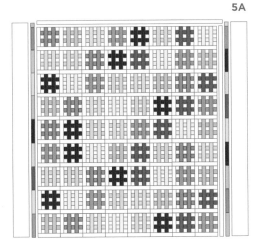

**5A**

**5B**

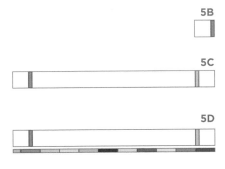

**5C**

**5D**

toward the print strips. Sew one to either side of the quilt with the print strips toward the inside as shown. **5A**

Cut (4) 5½" background squares and set aside for the moment. Sew enough 1½" print strips together until you have a strip that measures at least 22" long. From that strip, cut (4) 5½" lengths and sew one to each 5½" square. We'll call these corner blocks. **5B**

Now measure the quilt through the center horizontally, stopping when you reach the small, print pieced borders. Add ½" to that measurement and make (2) 5½" border strips that length (approximately 49½"). Sew a corner block to either end of the 5½" long border strip. **5C**

Sew enough 1½" print strips together to equal the length of the top and bottom borders (approximately 61½"). Sew a strip to one side of each border strip. **5D**

Sew one to the top and one to the bottom of the quilt. **5E**

Layer the quilt with backing and batting and quilts as desired. Square up and trim the excess batting and backing away. Add binding to finish. See the Construction Basics (pg. 100) for binding instructions.

**5E**

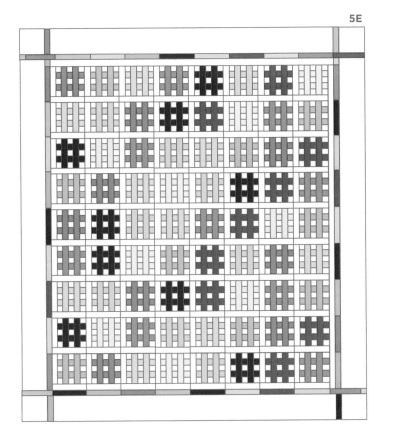

For the tutorial and everything you need to make this quilt visit:
www.msqc.co/blockfall15

# dresden squared

quilt designed by JENNY DOAN

Sometimes when starting a project, you have a picture in your head of how it's supposed to turn out, so you don't even think about other potential possibilities that might be better or more interesting. But if you give your imagination room to grow, amazing things can happen!

When our family moved from California to the farm in Missouri, our boys immediately started scoping out a spot for a treehouse. The boys had in their minds the exact configuration of four trees needed to make the greatest arboreal fort of all time, but they could only find three trees and were unable to match their original vision. So you know what they did? They cut down an old dead tree from another spot and dragged it

over to the other three. Then they dug a hole, braced the old dead tree into position, and cemented it into place. With their four trees ready to go, it was time for the real fun to begin.

The treehouse's base platform was about the only thing this tree fort would ever have in common with a traditional treehouse. Those boys were not the type to think inside the box, so they drew up plans and scoured the library for cool ideas to add to their masterpiece. When it was finished, this was a treehouse for the ages, boasting a fireman's pole, a seventy-five foot long zipline, and even a pulley system used to lower a basket down into the kitchen.

I'd fill the basket with snacks and drinks and send it back up to the kids.

Any treehouse can be the setting of wonderful afternoons filled with imagination and adventure, but I think this one was especially magical because the boys had worked so hard to make it unique. Creativity is an amazing thing. Within each of us is the ability to build something that is new and different - especially if we let our imaginations go wild - and I think that's pretty special.

Often we quilters see a quilt that we like, and we have the desire to make an exact replica: same pattern,

same fabric, same scale. And there's nothing wrong with that. Goodness knows I do it all the time! But sometimes it's so empowering to grab hold of those creative reins and take some chances. The Dresden's Squared Quilt marks a significant departure from traditional Dresden patterns. I mean, who chops the edges off of perfectly good dresden plates? I do! I hope you'll agree that, as is so often the case, this was a chance worth taking.

# materials

*makes a 45" X 54" lap quilt*

**QUILT TOP**
• 1 package 10" squares

**SASHING, CIRCLES, AND INNER BORDER**
• 1 yard

**OUTER BORDER**
• ¾ yard

**BINDING**
• ½ yard

**BACKING**
• 3 yards

**FUSIBLE INTERFACING**
• ¾ yard

**TEMPLATE**
• MSQC Layer Cake Dresden Plate Template

**SAMPLE QUILT**
• **For You** by Zen Chic for Moda

## 1 cut

Cut each square in half once through the center. From each half, cut five blades using the 5" Charm Square line on the MSQC Dresden Plate template. Flip the template each time you cut. Repeat for the other half. Put the 10 blades in a stack. **1A**

From the sashing fabric, cut:
• (15) 1½" x 8½" rectangles
• (7) 1½" x WOF strips – set aside

## 2 block construction

Pair two complementary stacks of 10 blades. Sew the blades together alternating the colors. After adding the last blade, close the last seam. Press all the

**1A**

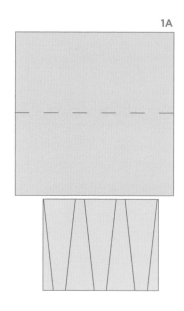

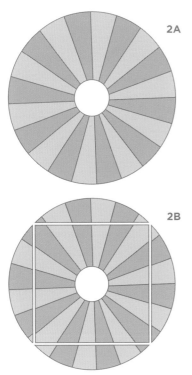

2A

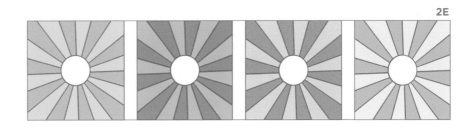

2E

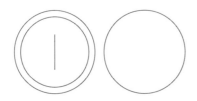

2B

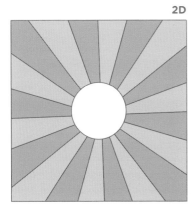

2D

seams in the same direction. **Make 20** blocks in this fashion. **2A**

Trim the blocks to an 8½" square. **2B**

Using the circle template provided on page 47, cut (2) 3½" circles, one from the fusible interfacing and one from the sashing yardage. Put the circles together with right sides facing and sew ¼" inside the outer edge.

**Note**: The bumpy side of the fusible interfacing will be facing toward the right side of the fabric circle. Make a slit in the circle made of interfacing just large enough to turn the circles right side out.
**Make 20**. **2C**

Turn the circles right side out. Press a circle to the center of each block and stitch in place using a decorative top stitch. A blanket stitch or a small zig zag will work nicely. **2D**

**Block Size**: 8" Finished

Sew the blocks together into rows of 4 with (1) 1½" x 8½" sashing strip between each of the blocks. Make 5 rows. **2E**

Measure the rows. Trim (4) 1½" sashing strips to this length (approximately 35½"). Sew the rows together with a sashing strip between each row.

## 3 inner border

Sew (5) 1½" strips of sashing together end-to-end to make one long strip. Trim the borders from this strip. Refer to Borders (pg. 100) in the Construction Basics to measure and cut the inner borders. The strips are approximately 44½" for the sides and approximately 37½" for the top and bottom.

## 4 outer border

Cut (5) 4½" strips across the width of the fabric. Sew the strips together end-to-end to make one long strip.

Refer to Borders (pg. 100) in the Construction Basics to measure and cut the borders. The strips for the sides are approximately 46½" long and the strips for the top and bottom are approximately 45½".

Layer the quilt with batting and backing and quilt. Square the quilt as you trim the excess backing and batting away. Add the binding to finish. See Construction Basics (pg. 101) for binding instructions.

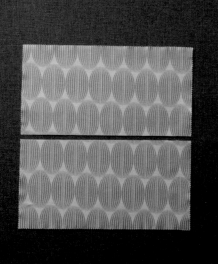

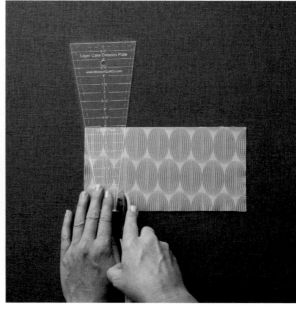

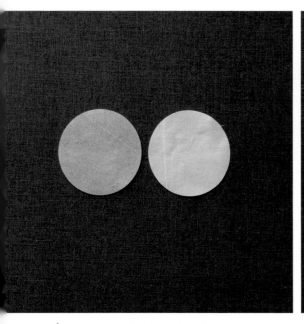

1 Cut each 10″ square in half. Step 1

2 From each rectangle, cut 5 blades using the 5″ charm line on the MSQC Dresden Plate template. Step 1

3 Sew 20 blades together. Step 2

4 Cut (2) 3½″ circles, one from interfacing and one from background fabric. Step 2

5 Sew the circles together with right sides facing. After they have been sewn, make a small cut in the interfacing and turn right side out. Step 2

6 After squaring the block, apply the circle and add sashing to one side of the block.

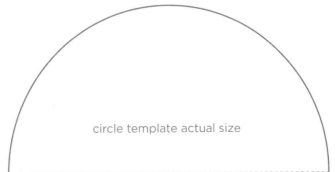

circle template actual size

*For the tutorial and everything you need to make this quilt visit:*
**www.msqc.co/blockfall15**

# easy
## cathedral
## window

table runner designed by HILLARY SPERRY

I love the Easy Cathedral Window block because it instantly makes me think of beautiful churches and cathedrals. Up at the top of my bucket list is a tour of the world's most famous churches. I'd love to see with my own eyes those gorgeous stained glass windows and feel the ancient reverence there. Of course, my first stop would have to be to Paris' Notre Dame.

Construction of the cathedral of Notre Dame began in the year 1160. Generations later, in the year 1345, the final touches were complete. I've never walked through those massive, ornate halls or gazed up at those world famous flying buttresses and stained glass windows, but from what I've seen, those 200 years of labor were totally worth it, to say the least!

There is something so special about a place of worship. You can just sense the love and sacrifice that went into creating a house of God. Here in Hamilton, Missouri, we may not have our own ancient cathedral, but we're pretty proud of our local churches. They are beautiful and sacred, and add so much to our community.

Years ago, the town held a big sesquicentennial celebration. We wanted to have a quilt show, but couldn't think of a suitable venue. Finally it was decided that the quilts should be displayed in our churches - not just one church, mind you, but all of the churches. The idea was that people would visit each of the churches to see the quilts, and by doing so they would also get to tour those beautiful old buildings.

The congregation of every church was responsible for their own quilt display, and I wondered how many quilts could be gathered by each. I admit that I was a little worried whether or not the quilt show would be successful, but when I started touring the churches, I was blown away by what I saw. Because folks felt comfortable in their own churches, they had brought out their most treasured pieces. Many of those quilts had never before been seen in public, and they were gorgeous!

That quilt show is still one of my warmest Hamilton memories. There are few things as precious to people as their churches and their heirlooms. To be able to share those with one another was a unifying and precious experiences for all of us.

“ There is something so special about a place of worship. You can just sense the love and sacrifice that went into creating a house of God. ”

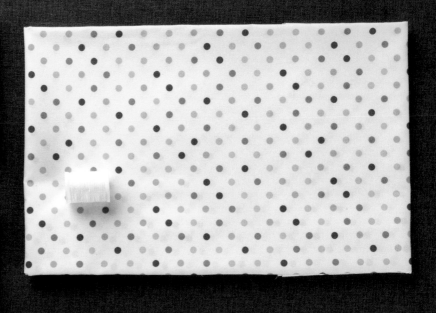

# materials

*makes a 27" X 18" table runner*

**TABLE RUNNER**
- 1 package of 5" solid-colored squares
- 1 package white 5" squares

**BACKING**
- ¾ yard
- 31" x 22" piece of thin batting

**BINDING**
- ¼ yard

**SAMPLE PROJECT**
- **Prairie** by Corey Yoder for Moda

# 1 fold and pin

Fold a white 5" square once on the diagonal wrong sides together and press. Pin the folded piece to a print 5" square. Remember, you are only pinning at this point. **1A**
**Make 16**.

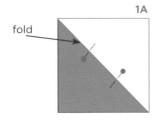

Fold 2 white 5" squares once on the diagonal and press. Pin the folded pieces to another square. The folded edges should butt up against each other. Again, you are only pinning, not sewing. **1B**
**Make 8**.

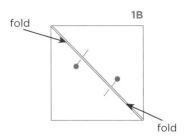

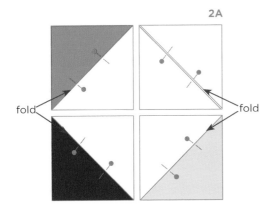

2A

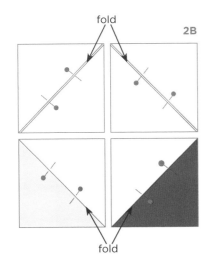

2B

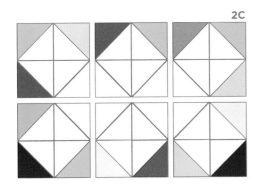

2C

3A

3B

## 2 sew

Sew 4 squares together. Three squares will have 1 folded white piece pinned in place, the remaining square will have 2 folded pieces pinned in place. Make 4 of these corner blocks and set aside for the moment. **2A**

Sew 4 more squares together. Two of the squares will have 2 folded piece pinned in place and 2 will have 1 folded pieces pinned in place. Make 2 inner blocks in this manner. **2B**

Sew the blocks together. The portion of the blocks that have the 2 folded pieces always goes toward the center of the runner. **2C**

## 3 finishing

From the backing fabric, cut:
- (1) 31″ x 22″ rectangle

Layer the backing (wrong side up) with the batting and the top of the table runner (right side up). Pin-baste the layers together. If you'd rather use spray baste, follow the manufacturer's instructions to hold the three layers together.

Place a 5″ colored square on point over each seam line. Pin in place. Roll the folded edges over each of the squares and top-stitch in place.  **3A**

After you have stitched around all the "window frames" **3B**, top stitch around the perimeter using a ¼″ seam allowance. Trim all excess batting and backing away. Add binding to complete the table runner.

1 Fold a white 5″ square once on the diagonal, press and pin to a print square. Step 1

2 Fold two white squares once on the diagonal and press. Pin to a print square. Step 1

Sew four squares together as shown to make a corner block. Step 2

4 Completed corner block. Step 2

5 To make an inner block, sew four squares together. Two will have two folded squares going toward the center and two will have one folded square going toward the outside. Step 2

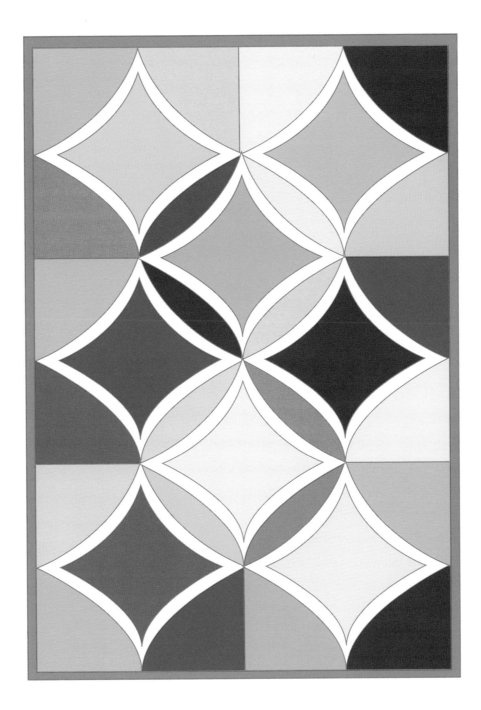

# everything
## bag

bag designed by SARAH GALBRAITH

My friend Alisa is the most prepared person I have ever met. If you're ever out and about and find yourself in need of a needle and thread, some headache medicine, or a roll of duct tape, just ask Alisa. I'm sure there's something in her purse.

I remember once when our children were small and we all went camping together. Those of you who have been camping with kids know that when you're headed to the wilderness with little ones, you have to plan for every possibility: extra pants in case someone has an "accident;" extra shirts in case someone spills stew down their front; extra blankets for when it turns out to be much, much colder than forecasted; and extra band-aids because everyone is going to end up with some sort of scrape or cut.

It's no easy thing to feel fully prepared to keep a crowd of tiny humans safe and comfortable in the mountains, but I've always

For the tutorial and everything you need to make this quilt visit: www.msqc.co/blockfall15

felt that it is important for children to spend time in nature, so I did my best to make it happen.

Bringing along other friends added to the fun of the trip, and Alisa was arguably my favorite camping partner. She came from a family of over-packers, and when she headed out on a wilderness adventure, everything but the kitchen sink went with her. So when our families camped together, instead of fretting over what to take and what to leave, I generally told myself not to worry about it; Alisa would have it. From can openers to bee sting kits, I felt comfortable leaving mine at home, because I knew that Alisa would be bringing one, two, or even three of hers.

When I first saw the Everything Bag, I thought of Alisa. This is the perfect bag for the friend who has everything and needs a bag in which to carry all of it! With this pattern, you can get two big bags out of one pack of forty 2.5 inch strips. If I were smart, I'd make one bag for her and one for me, and start carrying around all those little extras for myself. But by now I've learned that if I don't bring it, Alisa will. So maybe I'll make both bags for her . . . that way it will be easier for her to tote around enough supplies for all of us!

# materials

*makes a 20" x 18" x 3½" bag*

**BAG**
- (12) 2½" x 44" assorted print strips
- ½ yard print

**STRAPS AND LINING**
- 1½ yard solid

**ADDITIONAL SUPPLIES**
- lightweight batting

**SAMPLE QUILT**
- **Ink Blossom II** by Sue Marsh for RJR

## 1 cut

From the print, cut:

- (2) 9½" x 21" rectangles – pockets

From solid fabric, cut:

- (4) 6" x 41" strips – Piece the strips to make (2) 6" x 80" strips for the straps.
- (2) 24½" x 20½" rectangles for lining.

From the lightweight batting cut:

- (1) 22" x 46" rectangle
- (4) 1½" x 40" strips

2A

3A

4A

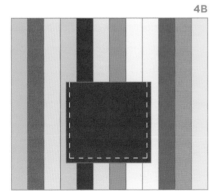

4B

## 2 straps

Press a solid strip in half lengthwise with wrong sides facing to create a center fold. Open the strap and press both raw edges so they meet at the fold. Press the strap in half again, so the raw edges are tucked into the fold.

Open one of the folded edges and place the 1½" strips of lightweight batting between the center of the strip and the fold. Rather than sewing the lightweight batting strips together, butt one length up to the first and so on. Stitch the strap closed ¼" from the edge.  Stitch two more lines along the length of the strap, once at the center point and once about ¼" from the outer edge. 2A

## 3 bag assembly

Lay out 12 assorted 2½" strips and stitch them together. 3A

Layer the batting rectangle and the sewn strips together and quilt. We quilted our bag by using rows of straight stitching parallel to the seams.  After the quilting is complete, cut the large rectangle in half and trim each side to 24½" x 20½".

## 4 pockets

Fold a pocket rectangle in half with the wrong sides facing. Press and stitch ⅛" from the fold. **Make 2.** 4A

Center a pocket on a Side Unit with raw edges of the pocket approximately 17½" below the top. Stitch the pocket to the Side Unit, then press the pocket up. Top stitch the bottom of the pocket through all layers. Pin the sides of the pocket in place. **Repeat** for remaining pocket and the other side. 4B

## 5 putting it together

Stitch one Side Unit and 1 lining rectangle at the top edge with right sides facing. **Repeat** for the other side.

While keeping the lining out of the way, place 1 strap over both pocket edges on one side of the bag. Before you stitch the strap in place, check to see if you need to adjust the strap length. After making any adjustments, top stitch the edge of the strap, starting from the bottom of the sides and stitching up to the lining seam. Stitch across the seam and down the other edge of the strap to the

5A

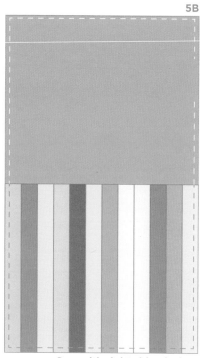

5B

Sew with right sides facing.

5C

1¾"

bottom edge. **Repeat** for the other side of the strap. 5A

In the same manner, stitch the remaining strap to the other side of the bag.

Place the two sides of the bag together with right sides facing. Match the quilted side to quilted side and lining to lining. Stitch all the way around the outer edge but leave a 4" opening on one side of the lining for turning. 5B

Refer to the Corner Diagrams and fold 1 side of the lining into a point on one bottom corner. Stitch 1¾" from the point as shown. Trim the corner ¼" away from the stitching line. Repeat for all the corners of the lining and bag. 5C

Turn the bag right side out through the side opening. Stitch the opening closed and tuck the lining inside of the bag.

Top stitch ½" from the edge all around the top of the bag.

For the tutorial and everything
you need to make this quilt visit:
**www.msqc.co/blockfall15**

# merry-go-round

quilt designed by HILLARY SPERRY

Back when we lived in California we weren't far from Santa Cruz, and in the summer there was a variety of awesome events out at the Boardwalk. We spent many fun evenings lounging on the beach, wandering the Boardwalk, and enjoying the stalls, games, and of course, the carousel.

The Looff Carousel, as it's called, was installed on the Boardwalk in 1911 by Danish woodcarver Charles I.D. Looff, and today it's a National Historic Landmark. It's a huge merry-go-round, covered in intricate, hand-sculpted details. Each horse is unique, from its flowing mane to its decorated bridle to the expression on its face, and every detail was carefully painted in a different gorgeous color.

As we awaited our turn, the kids loved examining the horses and picking their favorites. Heck, I liked to pick my favorite too, though I didn't throw a fit if I didn't get to ride on mine! I remember as the ride spun around you could grab a ring and try to throw it in a hole, and if you succeeded, your ride was free.

There aren't many carousels left that are as old and intricate as the one on the Santa Cruz Boardwalk. Riding on it was like taking a spin through the past.

As the summer wound down and the nights shortened, we visited the Boardwalk as often as we could, trying to soak up every last drop of summertime memories. I bet if I ever get back to the Santa Cruz Boardwalk and ride on that beautiful carousel again, I'll still be able to hear my little ones laughing and squealing as it spins.

I love this fun quilt because not only is it beautiful, but it reminds me of the nights we used to spend soaking up summer at the Santa Cruz Boardwalk and enjoying that gorgeous carousel.

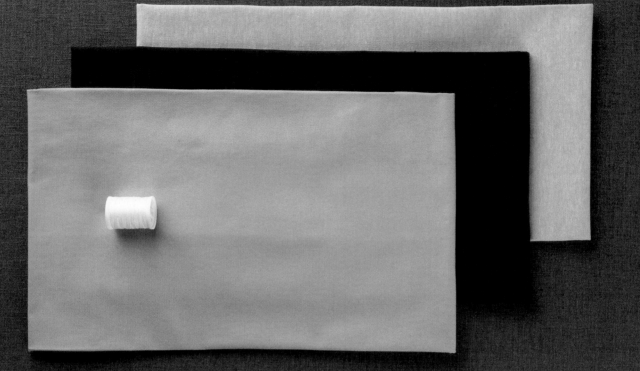

# materials

*makes a 56½" X 73½" quilt*

**QUILT TOP**
- 2¼ yards light background fabric
- 1 yard medium
- 1 yard dark or 5" print squares

**OUTER BORDER**
- 1¼ yards

**BINDING**
- ¾ yard

**BACKING**
- 3¾ yards

**SAMPLE QUILT**
- **Essex Yarn Dyed Linen-Flax** for Robert Kaufman, **Kona Cotton-Butterscotch and Navy** for Robert Kaufman

# 1 cut

From the light background fabric, cut:

- (13) 5" strips across the width of the fabric.

- Subcut the strips into 5" squares, for a total of 100. **Set aside 76 squares**.

- Subcut the remaining 24 into (4) 2½" squares for a **total of 96**. 1A

From the dark fabric, cut:

- (6) 5" strips across the width of fabric.

- Subcut the strips into 5" squares for a **total of 48**.

1A

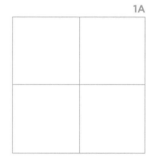

2A

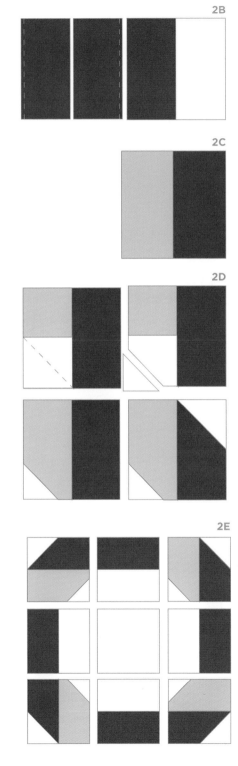

2B

2C

2D

2E

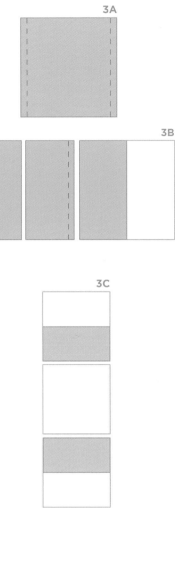

3A

3B

3C

From the medium fabric, cut:

- (6) 5″ strips across the width of fabric.

- Subcut the strips into 5″squares for a **total of 41**.

## 2 block assembly

Pair a background square with a dark square with right sides facing. Stitch along 2 opposite edges as shown. **Make 24.** 2A

Cut the stitched squares in half between the seams. Open each background/dark unit and press the seam allowance toward the dark fabric. You should have a total of **48 units**, each measuring 4½″ x 5″. 2B

In the same manner, make **48 units** using dark and medium squares. Trim these units to 4½″ square for the corners. 2C

Fold a background 2½″ square once on the diagonal with wrong sides facing. Press along the crease. This will be your stitching line. Prepare (88) 2½″ squares in this manner.

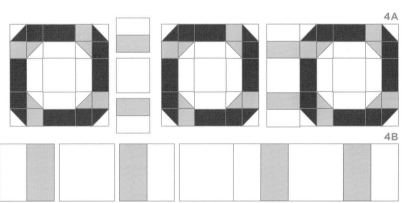

4A

4B

1 Sew a dark square to a background square as shown in diagram 2A. Cut the stitched squares in half between the seams.

2 Sew a dark square to a medium square as shown in diagram 2C. Cut the stitched squares in half between the seams. Open, press and trim to 4½".

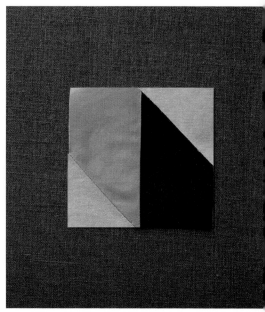

3 Stitch a 2½" background square to opposing corners of a dark/medium unit. **Note:** All of these units must be made the same way! Step 2

4 Sew the units together as shown. Step 2

5 Make sashing strips by sewing light and medium 5" squares together along the two outside edges. Cut the squares in half between the seam lines. Step 3

6 Add sashing strips between the blocks. Step 4

Open and stitch a 2½" background square to two opposing corners of a dark/medium corner unit.

**Note**: You must always sew the squares to the same opposing corners for all units exactly as shown.

Sew from corner to corner on the creased lines with right sides facing. Trim ¼" from the seam allowance as shown. **2D Make 48.**

Lay out (1) white 5" square, (4) background/dark units and (4) dark /medium corner units. Sew the units into rows of three and sew the three rows together to complete the block. **Make 12** following the diagram shown. **2E**
**Block size:** 12½" Finished

## 3 assemble sashing units

Pair a background square with a medium square with right sides facing. Stitch along 2 opposite edges as shown. **3A Make 17.**

Cut a stitched square in half between the seams as shown. Open each background/medium unit and press the seam allowance toward the medium fabric. You should have a **total of 34** sashing units. **3B**

Sew a sashing unit to either side of a background 5" square. **3C Make 17.**

## 4 quilt top assembly

Arrange the blocks and sashing strips into 4 rows, each made up of 3 blocks and 2 sashing strips. **4A**

Make a row of sashing by alternating 3 sashing strips with (2) 5" background squares. **4B Make 3.**

Sew the rows together beginning with a block row and alternate with a sashing row. **4C**

## 5 outer border

Cut (7) 5½" strips across the width of the fabric. Sew the strips together end-to-end to make one long strip. Trim the borders from this strip.

Refer to Borders (pg. 100) in the Construction Basics to measure and cut the outer borders. The strips are approximately 64" for the sides and approximately 57" for the top and bottom.

## 6 quilt and bind

Layer the quilt with batting and backing and quilt. After the quilting is complete, square up the quilt and trim away all excess batting and backing. Add binding to complete the quilt. See Construction Basics (pg. 101) for binding instructions.

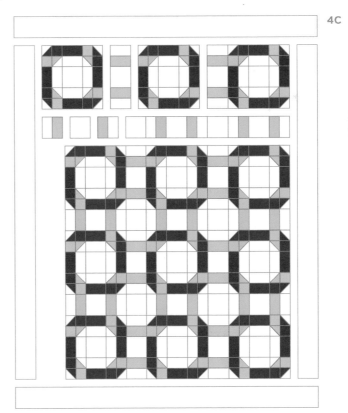

4C

# chevron
# blocks

quilt designed by JENNY DOAN

Back-to-school time brings back so many memories. It was such an exciting time as the kids anticipated new friends, new teachers, and of course, a few cute new outfits to wear to school.

I remember one particular first day of school when Sarah and Natalie were just five and six years old, respectively. Living out in the country required them to ride the bus to school. One morning we woke up to pouring rain and as I scrambled to find something to keep them dry, I reached into the closet and grabbed a bright yellow rain coat for Natalie. It had a hood and clasps on the front, and she looked so sunny and cute in it. For Sarah, though, I found a coat and hat ensemble that was covered in puppies, and had a tall pointy hood. I thought it was adorable, but fashion-conscious Sarah was not convinced. I used my motherly powers of persuasion to convince her that it was not too babyish and that she would look just fine. We zipped up the coat and raced out the front door just in time for the girls to hop onto the bus before it pulled away.

*For the tutorial and everything you need to make this quilt visit:*
**www.msqc.co/block1fall15**

I didn't give the raincoats another thought until Sarah tore into the house that afternoon, tears welling up in her eyes and anger surfacing through her face.

"Mom! I'm NEVER wearing this hat again! I CAN'T believe you made me wear such a stupid hat! A big boy on the bus called me a conehead!"

As Maternal Jenny, I ached for my daughter's hurt feelings, but as Mischievous Jenny, I admit I got a kick

out of her schoolyard drama. I may or may not have let out a little giggle, which only infuriated Sarah even more!

Childhood is full of learning experiences. Some make you laugh, some make you cry, but moment after moment, they all form you into the person you grow up to become. As devastated as Sarah was by that boy on the bus and his mean comment, that experience left a mark in her heart, and I'm certain

it had something to do with the kind and patient way Sarah speaks to others today. She knows firsthand how it feels to be on the receiving end of bitter or ugly words, and as a result, she is one of the gentlest, kindest women I know.

As difficult as it is to watch our children go through hard moments, it sure is rewarding to watch them bounce right back with an added measure of wisdom that can only come from experience.

# materials

*makes a 75" X 91" quilt*

**QUILT TOP**
- 1 package 10" print squares
- 1 package 10" background squares
  OR 3 yards cut into 10" squares

**INNER BORDER**
- ¾ yard

**OUTER BORDER**
- 1¼ yards

**BINDING**
- ¾ yard

**BACKING**
- 5½ yards

**SAMPLE QUILT**
- **Eden** by Tula Pink for Free Spirit Fabrics

## 1 block construction

Place a background 10" square atop a print 10" square with right sides facing. Draw a line from corner to corner twice on the diagonal on the reverse side of the background square. Sew ¼" on either side of the drawn lines. **1A**

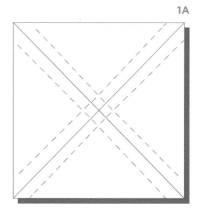

1A

Using your rotary cutter and ruler, cut through the center of the squares vertically and horizontally, then on each of the drawn lines. You will have 8 half-square triangles. **1B**

Open the half-square triangles and press the seam allowance toward the darkest fabric. Trim each half-square triangle unit to 4½". **1C**

76

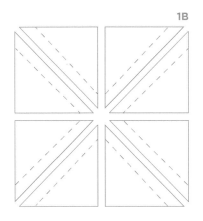

1B

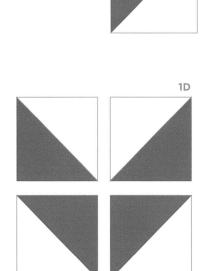

1C

1D

Sew four half-square triangles together as shown (on pg. 3) to make a block. **Make 80.** 1D

**Block size:** 8" Finished

## 2 layout and sew

Sew the blocks together in rows of 8. Make 10 rows. Press all odd numbered rows toward the right and all even numbered rows toward the left. 2A

## 3 inner border

Cut (8) 2½" strips across the width of the fabric. Sew the strips together end-to-end to make one long strip.

Refer to Borders (pg. 100) in the Construction Basics to measure and cut the borders. The strips for the sides are approximately 80½" and the strips for the top and bottom are approximately 68½".

2A

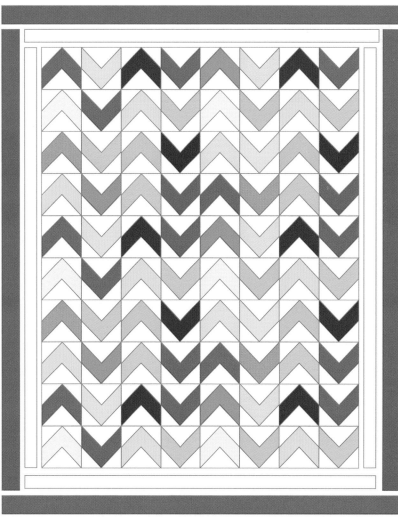

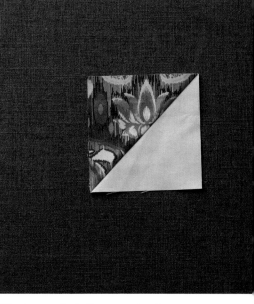

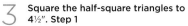

1   Layer a 10" print square with a 10" background square. Draw a line from corner to corner twice on the diagonal and sew ¼" on either side of the lines. Step 1

2   Cut the sewn squares through the center horizontally and vertically. Then cut along the drawn lines. Step 1

3   Square the half-square triangles to 4½". Step 1

4   Sew 4 half-square triangles together to make one block. Step 1

5   Sew the blocks together into rows. Step 2

## 4 outer border

Cut (8) 4″ strips across the width of the fabric. Sew the strips together end-to-end to make one long strip.

Again, refer to Borders (pg. 100) in the Construction Basics to measure and cut the borders. The strips for the sides are approximately 84½″ and the strips for the top and bottom are approximately 75½″.

## 5 quilt and bind

Layer the quilt with batting and backing and quilt. Square the quilt as you trim the excess backing and batting away. Add the binding to finish. See Construction Basics (pg. 101) for binding instructions.

For the tutorial and everything
you need to make this quilt visit:
**www.msqc.co/blockfall15**

# Xs and Os

quilt designed by JENNY DOAN

Like most of you, I didn't grow up with computers or email, so the mail that showed up in our box was an absolute treasure to me. Every year on my birthday I could be sure of getting a card in the mail from my Grandma Fish, and for years I saved them all in a shoebox under my bed. When I was feeling bored or blue, I would get out that old shoebox and look at the cards one at a time. My heart warmed as I read her messages written in beautiful cursive and saw again that Grandma had signed each card with plenty of Xs and Os beside her name. I knew Grandma loved me, and here were her hugs and kisses to prove it.

Today we have a generation that doesn't know how to write in cursive, let alone how to mail a letter, and they may soon forget how to write in English altogether! My grandkids send me plenty of texts, of course, but these days even short text messages seem to have words replaced by those teeny little pictures called emoticons. If you want to send someone a hug, you can send them an emoticon of people hugging. If you want to send a kiss, there's one of big red lips all puckered up.

I'll admit I love getting a hug from a grandchild, even it is in the form of a teeny digital image. But it does make me sad to think that kids these days have probably never received a card in the mail, and may not even know what "xoxo" means. You can't keep a text in a shoebox under your bed!

That's one of the reasons I love this quilt. It's packed from corner to corner with a special message of love for the person you're giving it to, made with love from beautiful fabric stitched with care. These hugs and kisses will comfort them for a lifetime.

" . . . packed from corner to corner with a special message of love for the person you're giving it to . . . "

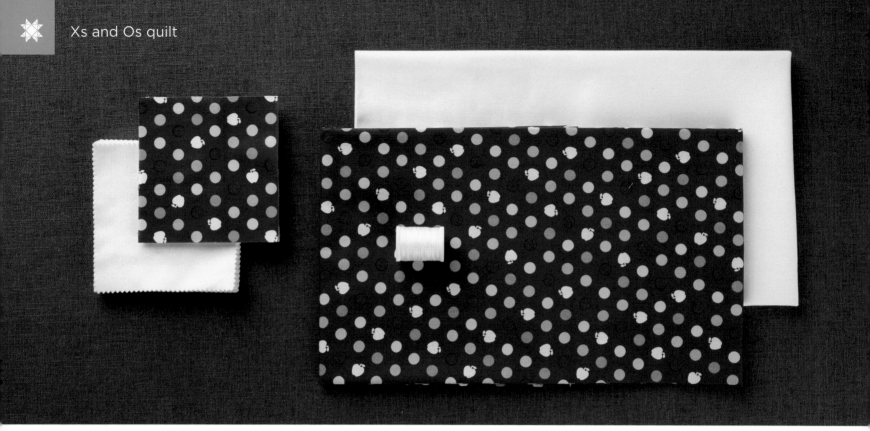

# materials

*makes a 68" X 77" quilt*

**QUILT TOP**
- (4) packages (42 ct.) 5" print  squares
- (2) packages (42 ct.) 5" white squares
  OR 1¾ yards cut into 5" squares

**INNER BORDER**
- ¾ yard

**OUTER BORDER**
- 1½ yards

**BINDING**
- ¾ yard

**BACKING**
- 4¾ yards

**SAMPLE QUILT**
- **Apple Hill Farm** by Kids Quilts for RJR

# 1 cut

Cut (84) white 5" squares in half vertically and horizontally for a total of (336)
2½" squares. **1A**

# 2 sew

Fold each 2½" white square once on the
diagonal and press. Sew a square to two
opposing corners of a print 5" square,
using the crease as the stitching line. **2A**
Trim the excess fabric ¼" away from the
seam line. **2B**

**Make 168 block units**.

**1A**

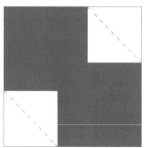

**2A**

## 3 block construction

Stitch (4) units together as shown (on pg. 3) to make one block.

**Make 42.** 3A

**Block Size:** 9″ finished

## 4 arrange and sew

Sew (6) blocks together to make a row.

Make 7 rows. Press the seam allowances in the odd-numbered rows toward the left and the even-numbered rows, toward the right. Sew the rows together.

## 5 inner border

From the inner border fabric, cut (7) 2½″ strips across the width of the fabric. Sew the strips together end-to-end.

Refer to Borders in Construction Basics (pg. 6) to measure and cut the borders. The strips are approximately 63½″ for the side borders and 58½″ for the top and bottom.

## 6 outer border

Cut (8) 5½″ strips across the width of the fabric chosen for the border.

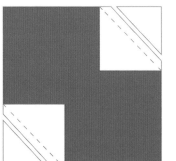

2B

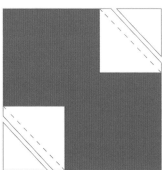

3A

1 Cut 5″ squares in half horizontally and vertically to make 2½″ squares. Step 1

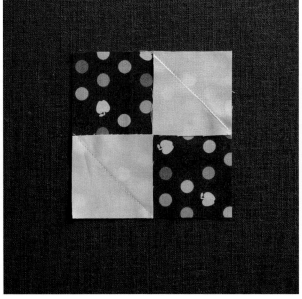

2 Sew a 2½″ white square on two corners of a print square. Step 2

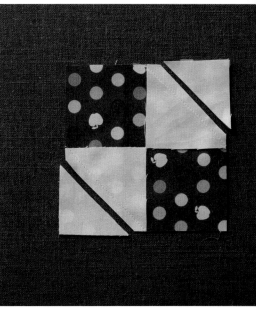

3 Trim the excess fabric away ¼″ away from the sewn seam. Step 2

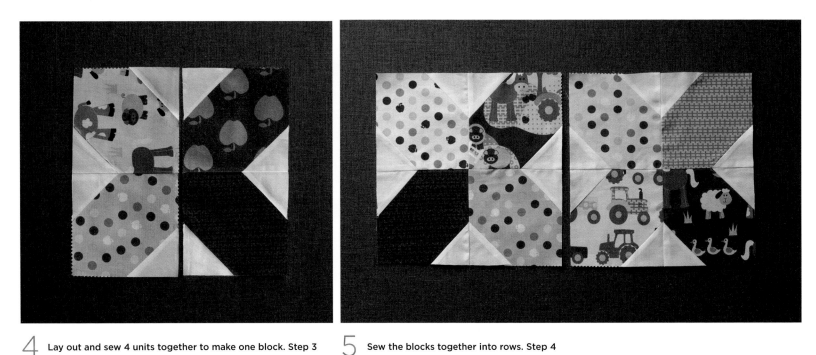
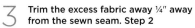

4 Lay out and sew 4 units together to make one block. Step 3

5 Sew the blocks together into rows. Step 4

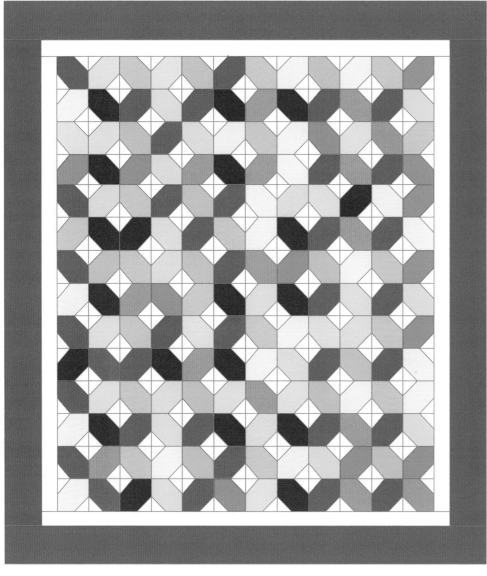

Sew the strips together end-to-end.

Refer to Borders in Construction Basics (pg. 100) to measure and cut the outer borders. The strips are approximately 67½" for the side borders and 68½" for the top and bottom.

## 7 quilt and bind

Layer the quilt with backing and batting. Quilt as desired. After the quilting is complete, square up the quilt and trim the excess backing and batting away. Add binding to complete the quilt. See Construction Basics (pg. 101) for binding instructions.

# Using Crossroads Denim

*Amy Barickman, founder of Indygo Junction and Amy Barickman.com has published nearly 1200 patterns and 80 books during her tenure in the fabric arts industry. Titles include Amy Barickman's Vintage Notions, Indygo Junction's Fabric Flowers, Dimensional Denim, and The Magic Pattern Book. Through her blogs, websites and e-newsletters, Amy inspires countless crafters to explore their own creative spirit and experiment with the newest sewing, fabric and crafting techniques. Keep up with Amy as she shares her ideas and inspiration at www.AmyBarickman.com and www. IndygoJunction.com.*

I want to tell you about one of my favorite fabrics, denim. This amazingly versatile textile originated in Nimes, France and was originally called serge de Nimes (de Nimes = denim, get it?). Yes, this American staple was founded in France.

Recycling materials today has become the norm, but when I published my Denim Redesign book in 2006, recycling was still on the fringes of sewing society. Since then I have created patterns that feature recycled denim whenever possible. Denim is a main-

stay for me because I love the fact that the fabric is so accessible. An average American owns 175 pairs of jeans in their life. Between family leftovers and thrift stores, it's easy for a beginner to find inexpensive fabric to work with. It is fascinating to me to explore creative ideas with each new denim project. To see which patterns offer a recycling option, look for the recycled logo on our patterns.

## Colored Crossroads

I love working with denim and for years, I was on the lookout for basic,

colored denim that could crossover from fashion to home. I also wanted something that would pair well with quilting cottons. I worked with James Thompson and Co. to develop a line of pre-shrunk and softened denim, which I branded Crossroads Denim.

Crossroads is a 58″ wide, 10 oz. denim available in 19 colors (with more coming). The softening technique used in production gives the fabric a beautiful drape. I named the line after the Crossroads neighborhood in downtown Kansas City (not too far from Hamilton!) which is an urban neighborhood going through an artistic renaissance. This inspirational district mingles utility with artistic vision, and reminded me of denim: a casual, utilitarian fabric, used for creative sewing.

I enjoy experimenting with Crossroads in a variety of projects - the fabric inspired me to create a special line of Crossroads patterns. This line includes everything from garments, like our Modern Silhouette Vest to home décor projects like our Banded Baskets.

## Fabric Manipulations

Crossroads Denim is ideal for working with fabric manipulation techniques. Ripping denim gives it a beautiful unfinished edge that you can use in techniques such as the Strip N' Stitch, which is featured in my book *Dimensional Denim*. Jenny and I used the Strip N' Stitch technique to create a Crossroads Quilt (look for the upcoming pattern!)

Stitching can add color and charm to an old denim jacket or jeans. Even just embroidering a solid design on a dark denim can add visual interest, as these examples from my book *Stitched Style* demonstrate. If you don't hand embroider, machine stitching can have the same effect. When topstitching or embroidering on denim, I love using Sulky's 12 wt. thread, although you can use any denim thread (a 16/100 needle is recommended for this heavier thread).

You don't need to have an embroidery machine to add interesting stitches to your denim, look no further than the decorative stitches that come with most machines. We like to cover fabric with different stitches, creating an embellished fabric. The stitches on my patterns, The Stitched Top Tote and the Petite Stitched Purse are found on most machines. Quilting can also add visual interest, as the asymmetrical designs on the cuffs and placket of the Cutting Edge Jacket shows.

Denim, both recycled and my own Crossroads, continues to be an inspiration as I design my new patterns; I am energized by all the project possibilities this fabric lends me. I can't wait to find new ways to use this durable and fashionable fabric.

# chevron block

**QUILT SIZE**
75" X 91"

**DESIGNED BY**
Jenny Doan

**PIECED BY**
Kelly McKenzie

**QUILTED BY**
Debbie Allen

**QUILT TOP**
1 package 10" print squares
1 package 10" background squares
   **OR** 3 yards cut into 10" squares

**INNER BORDER**
¾ yard

**OUTER BORDER**
1¼ yards

**BINDING**
¾ yard

**BACKING**
5½ yards

**SAMPLE QUILT**
**Eden** by Tula Pink for Free Spirit
Fabrics

**ONLINE TUTORIALS**
msqc.co/blockfall15

**QUILTING**
Variety

**PATTERN**
pg. 72

# dresden squared

**QUILT SIZE**
45" X 54"

**DESIGNED BY**
Jenny Doan

**PIECED BY**
Kelly McKenzie

**QUILTED BY**
LInda Frump

**QUILT TOP**
1 package 10" squares

**SASHING, CIRCLES, AND INNER BORDER**
1 yard

**OUTER BORDER**
¾ yard

**BINDING**
½ yard

**BACKING**
3 yards

**FUSIBLE INTERFACING**
¾ yard

**TEMPLATE**
MSQC Layer Cake Dresden Plate
Template

**SAMPLE QUILT**
**For You** by Zen Chic for Moda

**ONLINE TUTORIALS**
msqc.co/blockfall15

**QUILTING**
Champagne Bubbles

**PATTERN**
pg. 40

# easy cathedral window

**PROJECT SIZE**
27" X 18"

**DESIGNED BY**
Hillary Sperry

**PIECED BY**
Jenny Doan

**QUILTED BY**
Jenny Doan

**TABLE RUNNER**
1 package of 5"print squares
1 package white 5" squares

**BACKING**
¾ yard
31" x 22" piece of thin batting

**BINDING**
¼ yard

**SAMPLE QUILT**
**Prairie** by Corey Yoder for Moda

**ONLINE TUTORIALS**
msqc.co/blockfall15

**PATTERN**
pg. 48

# everything bag

**BAG SIZE**
20" x 18" x 3½"

**DESIGNED BY**
Sarah Galbraith

**PIECED BY**
Cindy Morris

**QUILTED BY**
Cindy Morris

**BAG**
(12) 2½" x 44" assorted print strips
½ yard print

**STRAPS AND LINING**
1½ yard solid

**ADDITIONAL SUPPLIES**
lightweight batting

**SAMPLE BAG**
**Ink Blossom II** by Sue Marsh for RJR

**ONLINE TUTORIALS**
msqc.co/blockfall15

**PATTERN**
pg. 56

# flutterby

**QUILT SIZE**
57" X 69"

**DESIGNED BY**
Natalie Earnheart

**PIECED BY**
Natalie Earnheart

**QUILTED BY**
Sherry Melton

**QUILT TOP**
(1) roll of 2½" strips

**BACKGROUND AND INNER BORDER**
1¼ yards

**OUTER BORDER**
1¼ yards

**BINDING**
¾ yard

**BACKING**
3¾ yards

**SAMPLE QUILT**
**Small Talk** by Studio E

**ONLINE TUTORIALS**
msqc.co/blockfall15

**QUILTING**
A Notion to Sew

**QUILT PATTERN**
pg. 24

# hashtag

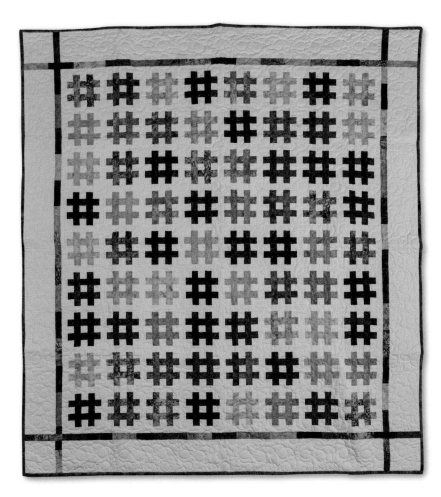

**QUILT SIZE**
61" X 67"

**DESIGNED BY**
Jenny Doan

**PIECED BY**
Cindy Morris

**QUILTED BY**
Debbie Allen

**QUILT TOP**
1 package 10" print squares

**BACKGROUND AND BORDERS**
3½ yards

**BINDING**
½ yard

**BACKING**
4 yards

**SAMPLE QUILT**
**Malam Batiks Blueberry Plum**
by Jinny Beyer for RJR

**ONLINE TUTORIALS**
msqc.co/blockfall15

**QUILTING**
Loops & Swirls

**PATTERN**
pg. 32

# indian
# summer

**QUILT SIZE**
70" X 87½"

**DESIGNED BY**
Jenny Doan

**PIECED BY**
Kelly McKenzie

**QUILTED BY**
Debbie Elder

**QUILT TOP**
(1) pack 10" print squares
(1) pack 10" background squares
     or 3 yards of background
     fabric cut into 10" squares

**BINDING**
¾ yards

**BACKING**
5½ yards

**SAMPLE QUILT**
**Tiger Lily** by Heather Ross for
Windham

**ONLINE TUTORIALS**
msqc.co/blockfall15

**QUILTING**
Little Nature

**PATTERN**
pg. 8

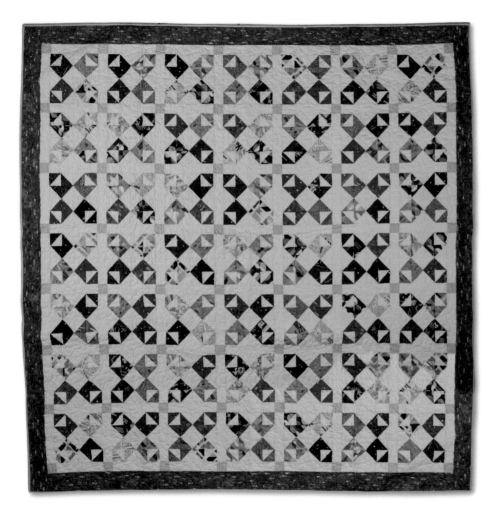

# love notes
# star

**QUILT SIZE**
82" X 94"

**DESIGNED BY**
Natalie Earnheart

**PIECED BY**
Carol Henderson

**QUILTED BY**
Emma Jensen

**QUILT TOP**
4 packs of 5" print squares
4 packs of 5" background squares
    **OR** 3 yards cut into 5" squares

**SASHING**
2 yards background

**CORNERSTONES**
½ yard

**OUTSIDE BORDER**
1½ yards

**BINDING**
¾ yard

**BACKING**
7½ yards

**SAMPLE QUILT**
**Story** by Carrie Bloomston/Such
Designs for Windham

**ONLINE TUTORIALS**
msqc.co/blockfall15

**QUILTING**
Heart Large

**PATTERN**
pg. 16

# merry-go-round

**QUILT SIZE**
56½" X 73½"

**DESIGNED BY**
Hillary Sperry

**PIECED BY**
Natalie Earnheart

**QUILTED BY**
Betty Bates

**QUILT TOP**
2¼ yards light background fabric
1 yard medium
1 yard dark or 5" print squares

**OUTER BORDER**
1¼ yards

**BINDING**
¾ yard

**BACKING**
3¾ yards

**SAMPLE QUILT**
**Essex Yarn Dyed Linen-Flax** for
   Robert Kaufman,
**Kona Cotton-Butterscotch and Navy**
   for Robert Kaufman

**ONLINE TUTORIALS**
msqc.co/blockfall15

**QUILTING**
Meander

**PATTERN**
pg. 64

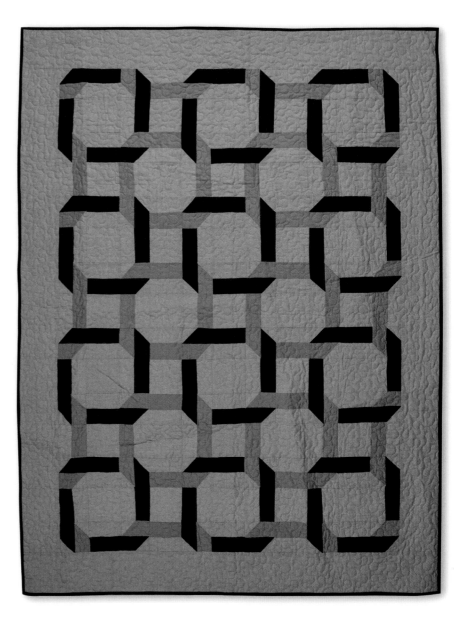

# Xs and Os

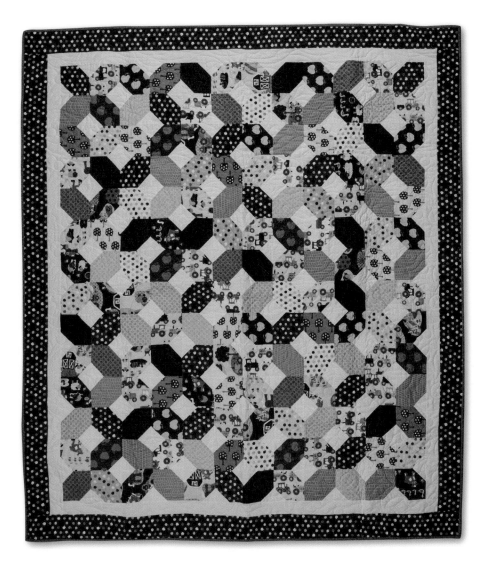

**QUILT SIZE**
68" X 77"

**DESIGNED BY**
Jenny Doan

**PIECED BY**
Jenny Doan

**QUILTED BY**
Karen Russell

**QUILT TOP**
(4) packages (42 ct.) 5" print
    squares
(2) packages (42 ct.) 5" white
    squares(2) **OR** 1¾ yards cut into
    5" squares

**INNER BORDER**
¾ yard

**OUTER BORDER**
1½ yards

**BINDING**
¾ yard

**BACKING**
4¾ yards

**SAMPLE QUILT**
**Apple Hill Farm** by Kids Quilts
for RJR

**ONLINE TUTORIALS**
msqc.co/blockfall15

**QUILTING**
Tractor

**PATTERN**
pg. 80

# construction basics

- All seams are ¼" inch unless directions specify differently.

- Cutting instructions are given at the point when cutting is required.

- Precuts are not prewashed; therefore do not prewash other fabrics in the project

- All strips are cut WOF

- Remove all selvages

- All yardages based on 42" WOF

**ACRONYMS USED**

| | |
|---|---|
| MSQC | Missouri Star Quilt Co. |
| RST | right sides together |
| WST | wrong sides together |
| HST | half-square triangle |
| WOF | width of fabric |
| LOF | length of fabric |

## pre-cut glossary

**5" SQUARE PACK**
1 = (42) 5" squares or ¾ yd of fabric
1 = baby
2 = crib
3 = lap
4 = twin

**2½" STRIP ROLL**
1 = (40) 2½" strip roll cut the width of fabric
    or 2¾ yds of fabric
1 = a twin
2 = queen

**10" SQUARE PACK**
1 = (42) 10" square pack of fabric: 2¾ yds total
1 = a twin
2 = queen

*When we mention a precut, we are basing the pattern on a 40-42 count pack. Not all precuts have the same count, so be sure to check the count on your precut to make sure you have enough pieces to complete your project.*

## general quilting
- All seams are ¼" inch unless directions specify differently.
- Cutting instructions are given at the point when cutting is required.
- Precuts are not prewashed; therefore do not prewash other fabrics in the project.
- All strips are cut width of fabric.
- Remove all selvages.
- All yardages based on 42" width of fabric (WOF).

## press seams
- Use a steam iron on the cotton setting.
- Press the seam just as it was sewn RST. This "sets" the seam.
- With dark fabric on top, lift the dark fabric and press back.
- The seam allowance is pressed toward the dark side. Some patterns may direct otherwise for certain situations.
- Follow pressing arrows in the diagrams when indicated.
- Press toward borders. Pieced borders may demand otherwise.
- Press diagonal seams open on binding to reduce bulk.

## borders
- Always measure the quilt top 3 times before cutting borders.
- Start measuring about 4" in from each side and through the center vertically.
- Take the average of those 3 measurements.
- Cut 2 border strips to that size. Piece strips together if needed.
- Attach one to either side of the quilt.
- Position the border fabric on top as you sew. The feed dogs can act like rufflers. Having the border on top will prevent waviness and keep the quilt straight.
- Repeat this process for the top and bottom borders, measuring the width 3 times.
- Include the newly attached side borders in your measurements.
- Press toward the borders.

## binding

*find a video tutorial at: www.msqc.co/006*

- Use 2½" strips for binding.
- Sew strips end-to-end into one long strip with diagonal seams, aka plus sign method (next). Press seams open.
- Fold in half lengthwise wrong sides together and press.
- The entire length should equal the outside dimension of the quilt plus 15" - 20."

## plus sign method

- Lay one strip across the other as if to make a plus sign right sides together.
- Sew from top inside to bottom outside corners crossing the intersections of fabric as you sew. Trim excess to ¼" seam allowance.
- Press seam open.

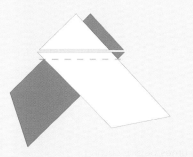

## attach binding

- Match raw edges of folded binding to the quilt top edge.
- Leave a 10" tail at the beginning.
- Use a ¼" seam allowance.
- Start in the middle of a long straight side.

*find a video tutorial at: www.msqc.co/001*

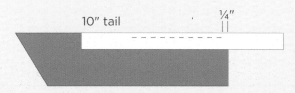

10" tail          ¼"

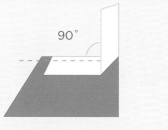
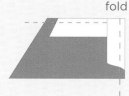

90°                              fold

## miter corners

- Stop sewing ¼" before the corner.
- Move the quilt out from under the presser foot.
- Clip the threads.
- Flip the binding up at a 90° angle to the edge just sewn.
- Fold the binding down along the next side to be sewn, aligning raw edges.
- The fold will lie along the edge just completed.
- Begin sewing on the fold.

## close binding

*MSQC recommends* **The Binding Tool** *from TQM Products to finish binding perfectly every time.*

- Stop sewing when you have 12" left to reach the start.
- Where the binding tails come together, trim excess leaving only 2½" of overlap.
- It helps to pin or clip the quilt together at the two points where the binding starts and stops. This takes the pressure off of the binding tails while you work.
- Use the plus sign method to sew the two binding ends together, except this time when making the plus sign, match the edges. Using a pencil, mark your sewing line because you won't be able to see where the corners intersect. Sew across.

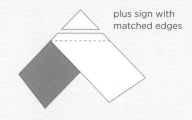

plus sign with
matched edges

- Trim off excess; press seam open.
- Fold in half wrong sides together, and align all raw edges to the quilt top.
- Sew this last binding section to the quilt. Press.
- Turn the folded edge of the binding around to the back of the quilt and tack into place with an invisible stitch or machine stitch if you wish.

# HIDEAWAY IN QUILT TOWN, USA

*PART 4*

## Smiling Service

——— *A JENNY DOAN MYSTERY* ———

*written by Steve Westover*

At the edge of town Jenny stood beside her tandem bicycle in the entrance to a used car dealership while Jin explained what brought her to Quilt Town, USA. Jin's story sounded plausible...kind of...yet Jenny felt uneasy about the woman's story. Something seemed "off". Jin dressed, spoke, and held herself with the grace of an educated professional, a stock broker, or maybe an advertising executive, so the gypsy tale she spun about traveling the country didn't add up.

"So you're just passing through?" Jenny asked. Jin bit at her lip and her eyes glanced toward a cloud overhead. Before she could fumble through what was about to be an obvious lie Jenny pressed on. "What are you really doing here, Jin?" Jenny's eyes narrowed and a sliver of a grin formed on her lips as she studied the woman like a prosecutor preparing to expose a perjured witness.

Jin's shoulder's slumped, her head lowered and she covered her face with her hands as a howl of fear, sadness, and pain seeped from between her fingers.

Jenny's eyes widened with alarm as she took a step back. She glanced to her left, and then her right, wondering who else might be witnessing this unexpected screech of emotion. Two cars passed on the road in front of them and a salesman from the auto dealership did an about face and sped off in the opposite direction. For all practical purposes Jin and Jenny were alone. Jin's head rose slowly and she removed her hands from her face as she looked up at Jenny with the expression of a lost child begging a stranger to help her find her mother.

The apprehension and unease Jenny had felt for Jin evaporated instantly. Jenny opened her arms and took a step toward her. Jin's body shrunk as she leaned into Jenny's arms. "It's okay, sweetie. Everything will be alright. Just cry it out," Jenny soothed, even though she had no idea what "everything" was.

Jin did. Another howl muffled against Jenny and then mingled with the breeze. Jenny held Jin tightly as tears soaked the shoulder of her blouse. When the crying subsided Jenny patted Jin on the back and in her most motherly tone said, "Let's talk." She motioned toward the tandem bicycle and Jin reluctantly climbed into a seat. Jenny climbed on beside her, turned the handle bars and waited for an opening before pulling onto the road. "Let's go, Jin. Pedal!"

When they arrived at the main shop Jenny left the bicycle out front and led Jin to the back office. Sitting across from each other at a quilting table Jenny leaned back and listened as Jin recounted her story. Jin told about the Chicago law firm where she worked, the spilled smoothie, and the two mysterious men who shot John Thurman. Jenny didn't speak. She couldn't. Her attention was rapt on Jin's harrowing story. When Jin concluded with her arrival in her Hamilton hideaway Jenny couldn't resist. She stood up and walked around the table, leaned down and gave Jin another bear hug.

"You can stay here as long as you want," Jenny said. She thought for a moment. "But you'll need a place to stay and you'll need a job."

Jin nodded in agreement. "In fact I was going to meet with..."

"I know of a cute place you can rent and you'll work for me," Jenny said excitedly. "Do you like to quilt?"

"Umm . . . it's just fabric and thread, right?"

Jenny smiled. "Not quite, but that's cute." Jenny thought for a moment and then continued. "First thing's first. We'll get you settled in a furnished apartment and then show you around the shops and warehouse."

"Warehouse?" Jin's tone made it sound like she was saying

"outhouse".

The hint of disapproval was evident to Jenny immediately. "Don't you worry, Jin. I'm not going to have you running a forklift or anything. In fact, I'm thinking you'd fit a little better upstairs in the customer service call center."

"Call center?" Jin's voice brightened with relief.

"Of course," Jenny said. "What better way to learn the basics of the quilting business than starting in customer service?" Jenny quoted a pay rate to which Jin agreed, and then Jenny pulled out her phone and dialed. "MK, what are you doing right now?" She listened and then frowned. "Oh, yeah. Our Columbia event. I forgot."

Jenny held the phone away from her ear as the cacophony of MK's "I told you so" and laughter nearly punctured her ear drum.

"MK, drop everything and meet me out front in five minutes. Yes, yes. I'm still going to Columbia but your plans have changed. There's someone I'd like you to meet." Jenny placed the phone in a pocket and then put a hand on Jin's shoulder. "MK's my assistant. She's going to take care of everything. Just don't trust her fashion advice."

***

After getting situated in an apartment above the sandwich shop, MK drove Jin past the warehouse and call center. "Be here at 9:30 tomorrow morning. Do you have a car?"

"I. . .uh."

MK grinned. You hardly need one in Hamilton but it would be a longish walk. Don't worry. I've got the perfect solution."

"Thank you, MK. You're very kind," Jin said.

MK brushed the words away with her hand. "Now it's time for a little fun. Jenny said you'll need some clothes and personal items. There's not much close by so we'll have to drive but there's a cute boutique where I shop. You'll love it."

Jin glanced at MK's plaid shorts with a chain stretching between the front pockets and the striped pastel blouse beneath the leather halter jacket. Yellow Chuck Taylors and green knee-length socks punctuated the ensemble.

"Sounds interesting," Jin lied. With no further explanation MK took Jin and Jenny's credit card shopping.

***

Thursday morning was a blur. After riding the tandem bicycle to the warehouse/call center at the edge of town, Jin met MK for a blitz tour of the facility before starting her duties.

Inside the football field length warehouse Jin's eyes wandered up and down the steel shelves stocked from floor to ceiling with fabrics of every assortment. A slender man rode what appeared to be a kind of new-age skateboard with a flexible joint in the middle. He glided expertly down the long rows on his RipStick, scanning boxes and pulling product for inspection. Jin scratched the back of her head while trying to take in the full scene without falling behind MK's brisk pace.

"Come on, Jin. This way," MK said as she pushed through a doorway of clear plastic slits leading into the shipping bay. A dozen shippers loaded their carts before returning to workstations to write personal messages thanking their customers. Jin was aware that MK was still talking but she wasn't listening. Stopping near one of the shipping stations Jin leaned in to study the workstation and then glanced down an adjoining row full of bins loaded with sundry products. "Jin."

Jin's attention drew toward the sound of MK's voice. She looked around for a moment until she spotted MK fifteen yards away standing at the base of a staircase. "Sorry," Jin said before rushing toward her docent. "I'm impressed," Jin said, but this time MK wasn't listening.

"The call center is upstairs. I'll have Sean show you around. He's Jenny's son."

Jin nodded. "Okay."

MK's lips straightened with focus before she continued. "I may have forgotten to tell him you were starting today and Jenny's out of town, so don't be surprised if he's a little...well..."

At the top of the stairs a vast room full of cubicles came into view. Each booth was waist-high with cheerful operators receiving calls while staring at computer monitors.

"It's true what they say, a smile can be heard," MK said as she flashed a goofy grin. A conference room, restrooms, and a break room were all positioned at the east side of the building.

"That's Sean over there," MK said, pointing to a lanky man wearing a tattered hoodie and a grizzly beard. "Wait here."

As MK rushed off to break the news to Sean that he'd be training a new employee, Jin navigated the cubicles, her eyes focused upon the wall at the other side of the room. A twelve foot long observation window looked down onto the main warehouse floor. She stood and watched the workers glide through the maze of crates and shelves like fish through coral reef.

"Jin."

Jin turned to see MK motioning for her to come. MK smiled broadly, seeming to enjoy Sean's grumpiness.

Sean removed a Bluetooth earpiece and then extended a hand for the obligatory shake. Jin grabbed it. "Thank you for this opportunity, Sean. You won't be disappointed you hired me."

"Of course not," he said. "*I* didn't hire you."

"Be nice," MK chided. "Jenny did." He nodded, accepting his speedy defeat. "Jin, you have a wonderful day. There's a lot to learn. Soak up as much as you can and don't worry if it takes you a few days to get the hang of things. Maybe we can get together at J's for a burger after work," MK said. "My treat."

"Great," Jin agreed.

Sean logged into a workstation and invited Jin to sit. He demonstrated how to navigate the service site as well as the incoming call controls. He put his earpiece in and set his iPad beside a headset on the desk. "Just play around in the systems for a little bit. Get familiar and then I'll have you sit with Grace so you can watch and listen to her for the rest of the day. Everything you say, I hear," he said motioning toward his earpiece. "And I see everything you see, and more," he said picking up his iPad. Just remember that and I'm sure you'll do great. Ask me any questions you have and we'll try to ease you into taking

calls when you're ready; probably tomorrow."

Jin nodded. "Got it."

And she did. Jin quickly read about the service standards for shipping and accuracy and then moved on to study customer order screens. She glanced at Sean who stood focused beside a cubicle, watching and listening to one of the service representatives. Toggling to another screen on her monitor she stared at the call initiation. Even though Sean had told her she would shadow another representative after she'd had time to explore the shipping, ordering and tracking systems, Jin couldn't bear the thought of sitting and watching all day long. She put on the telephone headset and opened her system to accept calls. She took a deep breath as her stomach fluttered in anticipation. A green box at the corner of her screen blinked so she clicked it with her mouse. "Thank you for calling Missouri Star Quilt Company customer service. This is Jin. How may I serve you?"

Jin listened to the customer's concern before navigating to the order screen and then the shipment tracking via the US Postal Service. "Mrs. Jackson, I see that your shipment was scanned at the Albuquerque North post office yesterday evening at 7:22 pm. It is out for delivery today so you should receive it this afternoon. I'm happy to see it should arrive within the standard seven day shipping window. How may I further assist you?" Jin listened. "Thank you for your business, Mrs. Jackson. Have a wonderful day." Jin clicked on the box at the top of her screen, disconnecting the call before putting her system on hold. She took a deep breath, readied herself and then took another call...and then another until she got into a rhythm.

Before she knew it, Jin was not only having fun but she also felt reconnected to the world. After only a few days without a phone, internet, or contact with anyone in her real life, Jin felt rejuvenated by the reality that an entire world still existed outside of her quilting hideaway in Hamilton. And the world was only a mouse click and a phone call away.